Snapshots in Eternity

Snapshots in Eternity

Stitching Together the
Four Corners of Existence

Jeffrey C. Starbuck

River Sanctuary
PUBLISHING

Snapshots in Eternity
Stitching Together the Four Corners of Existence
Copyright © 2012 by Jeffrey C. Starbuck

Cover design by Jessica Moreno

Author photo by Jayadeva Mandelkorn

ISBN 978-1-935914-22-8

Printed in the United States of America

Additional copies are available from:

www.jeffreystarbuck.com

Library of Congress Control Number: 2012938632

RIVER SANCTUARY PUBLISHING
P.O Box 1561
Felton, CA 95018
www.riversanctuarypublishing.com
Dedicated to the awakening of the New Earth

for Lila and Noah

and

also

David

CONTENTS

I

am

the

bottomless

pond

the

Beloved

hides

Herself

in

INTRODUCTION

A few comments may be helpful for many readers, here in the beginning, to increase your appreciation and enjoyment of this book. Any who wish to go directly to the poems are abundantly encouraged to do so, also. Return here later. Zig-zag back and forth. Weave in and out. Find your own path through the Garden because you'll always end up in the right place, which happens to be right here, although "right here" may not mean here at the end of the first paragraph in this Introduction.

The English word "taste" appears in a number of the poems. Also, "one taste" and other variations. The Sanskrit words *samarasa* and *ekarasa* mean "one taste," "single taste," "same taste." These terms are used in various ancient Hindu and Buddhist texts, including the Upanishads and the Tantras, as one way of describing the direct experience of Absolute Truth, the Awakened State, in which there is an undifferentiated unity, a perfect equanimity, and an unbounded harmonious bliss. For example, one can read, in these archaic texts, expressions such as: Ultimate Reality, when fully and directly apprehended, is "of one taste." (Please note, also, that the Tantras, referenced above, are a set of serious philosophical, spiritual scriptures and have little to do with an unfortunate knee-jerk connotation to that word in the "modern" world.)

"Spiritual" hunger, longing or yearning begins to develop once one has begun to "awaken." In the poems there are frequent references to this desire, this appetite, this developing "passion." This "spiritual passion" parallels a type of increasing "dispassion" for "worldly things." The Sanskrit word *vairagya* means "detachment, renunciation, freedom from worldly passion."

I purposely juxtapose "dispassion" and "passion" here. As to "passion," a certain energy and enthusiasm seems to be exuded by truly spiritual people. Look for a "mad," mischievous gleam, a twinkle in the eye. Listen for deep belly, whole body laughter. Modern or "post-modern," evolved (evolving), non-denominational,

1

non-sectarian spirituality is all about a complete involvement in the full spectrum of human activity, at least anything that is positive, life-affirming, generally considered to be "good" and not causing any harm. This complete involvement, by the way, is some good part of the real meaning of the term "tantra" ("tantric").

On the other hand, the spiritual path necessarily involves discipline, together with a practiced detachment from and non-clinging to outcomes, a certain type of "renunciation." The Bible verse "When I was a child, I spake as a child, I understood as a child, I thought as a child; but when I became a man, I put away childish things" refers to this discipline, this non-attachment, this state of vairagya.

We are to **up-level** our "attachments." To make them "preferences." We can "prefer" a particular outcome, so long as we don't get "bent out of shape" if it doesn't occur. It's fine to prefer a sunny, low wind day for our summit climb of Aconcaqua, or for the outdoor wedding, but we want to be able to maintain our sense of inner poise and balance if we don't get it. **Preferences** are preferred, are okay, are expected, aren't troublesome. Attachments result in yuckiness, in not feeling good, in being unbalanced and having unhappy disgruntled human relationships.

The idea is that our center of gravity is **inside** us; that we are defined by something "within" and not by anything on the outside. The outer trappings can be there, no problem; but there's not a rigid attachment to them. It's "being in the world but not of it." It's **that** space!

Everything in this dimension of Form, which means **everything** in what we call "reality," and this includes ghosts, glaciers and galaxies, is constantly changing, albeit at different rates. It's all **transforming**; it's all steadily becoming different than it was before. This is where Jesus steps in to advise us to "lay not up for yourselves treasures upon earth, where moth and rust doeth corrupt, and where thieves break through and steal."

Thus, are we passionate or dispassionate? It seems to be the right mingle of both! Furthermore, we begin to come right up against the limitations of language here, the point where language loses its ability to be useful. The same word can be used by two people in fundamentally different and opposite ways. Wars are waged because people don't understand what other people are saying, and they don't understand that they don't understand!!

Additionally, the use of "non-denomination, non-sectarian" above is not at all meant to imply that one can't or shouldn't follow one's chosen Sikh or Christian or Buddhist or Muslim (Sufi) or Jewish or Native American or Shaivite or Yogic or Shamanistic or any other path and set of beliefs and practices. It *is* necessary to be committed to something, to some practice at any given time, even if not calling it by a particular name and even if the commitment evolves over time. But we're certainly not looking to blend all the vegetables into one homogenous brew. That would leave the world colorless and without taste. "Reality" is a dimension of specificity and difference, many colors, shapes, sizes. There's plenty of room for everyone and everyone's individual choices and preferences. Just remember to be respectful of **all** others at **all** times, also.

We human beings are an intersection of the vertical and the horizontal. We are the way God expresses and knows ItSelf. We are both the ALL and the particular, the specific. Each of us is a totally unique being, the likes of which has never appeared in Form before, and will never appear again. As such, we each have a special set of gifts and talents to deliver to the world. **And**, at exactly the same time, we are this Formless Consciousness, this boundless Love, this Eternal Presence, this Quantum Field of Potentiality that is endlessly expressing new versions of ItSelf.

This is actually true of **all** of Creation, but we seem to be alone in the ability to be self aware (to be the "Witness") and to make conscious, as opposed to automatic, decisions; to experience awakened attention and to be intentional about "where" we point it! We are the ones "made in the image and likeness of God," which means that we are to do what God does. We are to create, at our level of resolution, our lives and worlds. We are to speak the Word, to think things into existence, to be **intentional** about the use of our **attention**! And what a job we've done!

Let me add, apropos the above, that there's a built-in protective code firmly embedded in the "software" of all Reality. Anything we desire, create, "think" into existence must be in tune with, in harmony with, everything else. We have to be "moving in the same direction" that "the Universe is moving." If we're out of sync, whatever we're creating won't and can't continue to work. We'll be out of balance and it won't be fun. Something will fall on our head! Our house will tumble! Harmony is intrinsic to the Cosmos.

This is not the place to discuss how or why things seem to have gotten very, very unbalanced and toxic here on Earth (to the degree that they have), nor is it the time to defend why we humans are different than dolphins, dogs and redwood trees. I will state that "the dominion we've been given over the earth" doesn't mean we are to rape, pillage, burn down and pollute. We have dominion in the same way you have dominion over your backyard flower garden. You take care of your garden, as a way to experience Beauty, Joy, Order and Harmony. Only now, the whole planet and everything on, in or above it is your (and everyone else's) backyard flower garden, so best to treat it all (and everyone else) accordingly.

The "heart cave" or "cavern" refers to the "spiritual heart," the heart center, Anahata Chakra. This is variously referenced throughout all of the world's sacred traditions. It is the "secret place of the most high." The red heart you see painted on Jesus and Mary's chests in Eastern Orthodox murals. Hanuman pulling the skin and surface of his chest away with both hands to reveal Ram and Sita enthroned there in the Center. The frequent use of the expression "Sacred Heart" in the Catholic world. Many illumined spiritual teachers have spoken glowingly of the wonders, the splendor of dwelling in "the Heart."

Those who have experienced It directly speak of a vastness, a spaciousness *in there*. It's a *cavern*, a secret holy place of mysteries, an inner or upper *room*, a "closet," insulated from the outer world of manifestation.

Please go find *It*. Once you've located *the Way*, go *there* frequently! Begin living from *there* always!

As you do, you'll find that you're ever right **HERE**, in the midst of an Eternal Presence that is your most loyal friend.

I was so thrilled the other day to learn that God
(just like an adoring grandmother) has a photograph
of me (and you too) on Her refrigerator!
And in Her wallet!
I've been eagerly awaiting the opportunity to
share this exciting news with you, the reader.

Thus, the following special feature has
been added at the very final moment.

When you find the perfect angle at which to turn this book so
that it catches the first rays of the early morning Sun, rising above
the horizon, you will perceive an absolutely immense holographic
reflection of the unbounded Joy
God feels upon living in and through you!

Have you ever seen the Creator dancing as
He Sings the Cosmos into Existence?
If not, you will!

You'll barely know what to do
once this Song starts Singing as you!

The "Acknowledgements" page, ordinarily found at the beginning,
can be seen after the "Notes" section at the end.
Life is meant to be unpredictable and FUN!!!

ETCHED...

Etched

on   the

back   side

of   all   surface,

Yahveh's

signature

mischievously

winks!

TAP DANCE   (Creation Story)

The word "ABSURD" walked up to me.

He tipped his hat; he tap-danced free.

He turned into a joyful storm

and made me feel within, quite warm.

He taught me how to laugh with glee

and painted such grandeur, a tree!

He planted deep inside of me

a sprouting seed

whene'er there's need.

Then, disappeared into a PUFF !

And now is seen in all the STUFF

that fills this world we call our home.

Please bow to Him as you do roam.[2]

ON THE DESKTOP, GOD IS WAITING

On the desktop, God is waiting.
She is very near.
She does choose to serve you.
You are quite, quite dear.

She is so, so eager,
Like the puppy's tail wag.
She is so, so happy,
When we find Her tag.

Let us come to open
To the ocean and the breeze,
For Her breath blows freely,
Even as we sneeze.

We do think we're separate.
How that makes Her sad.
For then the time comes close
To when we all might think we're bad.

Even though this "badness"
Is truly good manure.
Just need now to compost,
Very close to cure.

Guide into the Garden,
Guide me through to BE.
Grant that I may know my hand
As I sew me to Thee.

I so wish to finish
With this "I" I think is me.
I do want to harvest such.
Please do offer key.

Tell me when the end is near,
Or don't, as case may be.
For who would ever guess the time
When shoreline meets the sea.

May I know Your mercy, please.
May I know Your glee,
Even if this short appeal
Is so silly, wheeeeee!

Let me now set down this pen.
Let me hail the sun.
Let me harvest pearls galore,
Til pearls weigh a ton!

If this is truly corny,
If this is really queer,
Hear my entreaty anyway.
I know You will not jeer.

One day you will step INSIDE,
You who read these words.
You will hear the music.
You will sing the birds.

Then it is that you will know
Just how sweet the taste,
Of Great Mother's blessing,
Quite at ease, no haste!

And when it is you glimpse Her,
And when you will be near,
It is not up to you, oh no,
Yet there's no cause for fear!

Just always know that we are One,
Unbounded, blissful, free.
And you will know your destiny,
To kneel at Her knee.

THE DAMAGE CAUSED BY GOD

I've not been reading Hafiz,
Shams-ud-din Muhammad of Shiraz,
in this book of wild, honey-sweet poems.
I've been reading D. Ladinsky and H. W. Clarke, translators.
Also Meher Baba, Goethe and Ralph Waldo Emerson.
All the ancestral streams feeding Ladinsky, fueling Clarke,
gurgling up through Goethe, Emerson, Baba.

Hafiz may have uncovered a cascade, but from what
Source do waters infuse his wellspring?

I'm afraid I may be etching into my own soul, or that invisible
Friend who lives in the sky, the cave, the robin and the dolphin.
A blind rabbit pawing along the braille path,
returning to the succulent carrot Garden.

I'm digging back through these abandoned earth tunnels,
collapsed jungle passageways, overgrown canals and
lost secret gardens of my sinews and synapses.
All the evidence the big Moon has left,
scattered about for my delight.
A mystery about to be fathomed.
A thriller primed to startle its devotees.

We   are   pilgrims.
We're all circling Mt. Kailas.[3]
We all cast our nets out, gambling for the big Catch.

My mouth is so full,
that,   to open,
will initiate a
flood that'll sweep all the miles to the Sea.

I must return now to that Altar in my den,
to inquire of the Doctor who deals in
thunderstorms and maelstroms.
Forgive me now, I beg.

A SECRET ONE

There is a Secret One inside.

She spins the spiders' webs
and causes stars to form.

This Milky Way you call your own
is but a twinkle in Her eye.

Shout out Her Name continually
and She will kiss you on the mouth.

You will never want another.

You will wander   Wild !

SINCE ENERGY IS MATTER

Since energy is matter
and all matter is ever shifting form;
since no form is the final form,
with all form so intricately interdependent
that the original stitch cannot be seamless seen,
it makes little sense to script these truths into poetic verse.
Whatever can be stated, has already been.
And oh how sweetly!

Yet still, the urge arises,
a lust to fling fountain into sky,
to cast these spinning, bounteous visions into shape beholdable by all,
glimmering in the rainbow, snowflake and lilting northern lights,
congealing with such passion
that all creatures are propelled onto their feet,
then moved in dance so lustrous,
that the throat sings "Hallelu"!

Breathing in a huge lungful of the precious air surrounding you,
an ancient yearning will tremble in your chest.
Your shoulders, thighs and rib cage are immanent to burst.

Do you recall the Big Bang?

You've been chosen to host a wild-ass party,

brighter

                              and more lush!

THE ONE TASTE OF ALL LINES CONNECTING

There are times when the Immensity of Truth
"threatens" to come flooding into my day.
IT is always there, very close, right behind the
'seems' of existence, just on the other side of the
main support wall that holds up the house.
Insufficient are words in English to portray
IT's sweeping array of colors and shapes;
tastes, memories and aspirations;
the texture of desire and dimension.
Best maybe to set down the pen and enter into
Communion.

I'll drop by very early in the morning so
we can run along the high cliffs overlooking the Ocean,
Sun rising so gloriously
filling up the sky as it does perfectly,
entering all the cracks and small places
'til no space remains between anything.
That's the way the holy books always describe this world,
painted as if it were really truly
PRESENT...

VACATION IN THE COUNTRY

I will turn my cell phone off early this evening.

The Moon is nearly full and

one can easily view all of today's top stories,

streaming across its surface,

no reading glasses required.

Besides, that number the katydids are singing,

it's not a cover,

is it!

MEAL PRAYER, BUDDHIST SANGHA

This whole galaxy is food.

Everything at every imaginable level both eats and is eaten,

from spiral nebulae to the drunken ecstasy of your

sub-atomic particles spinning.

These cycles endlessly churn and circulate,

but never mind such polite babble,

for I have an absolutely voracious appetite tonight!

As do all those surrounding me in this circle of fellow travelers

I see as I look around into their eyes.

All are ravenous,

for revelation and wonder,

awakening and the emerging desire for the one true taste.

I now sit poised to eat this entire universe,

as too do those surrounding me.[4]

Let the show now begin!

SURFER

every day you get another opportunity to fly

each morning you can dive off the tip of your forehead,
deeply into the Big Dipper
and emerge up through the froth of the Milky Way

with every afternoon turn in the Amazon River,
unanticipated wonder will leap forth toward you

simply get your tickets from the mouths of the jaguars
guarding the gates to the overgrown jungle temple

wiggling new puppy excitement is being propagated by the
clandestine overnight romance of thymus and adrenals

the very best of Beethoven is being performed,
promiscuously erupting through the pores of your
forearm, inner thigh and cheek

the word on the street arrives as
Mayan Morse code magic
with its synaptogenic poetry

a lazy man once whispered into my ear,
"there's **nothing**
            you need to do **first**
                        in order to be enlightened"

on the other hand,

there's report of a silver surfer who rides every breath
you've ever taken,

tirelessly
                              since your birth,

in and out,
in and out,
that endless summer, end on end [5]

please locate this tiny person,
the same way you sift through random articles of clothing
on the tables at the annual church rummage sale
searching for that rare perfect find

in the center of the surfer's brow
lies the progenitor of the
world's most precious diamond,

with your name

ETCHED

across its glitter

INTELLECTUAL PROPERTY

To your right on the next barstool,
God sits doubled over in laughter.
He points to the palm of his right hand
where your eyes view swirling shifting fog
that congeals into a courtroom scene,
attorneys animatedly arguing on behalf of their clients.

Affectionately, he places his left arm around your shoulders
and, while beaming with enjoyment, articulates the
latest antics of those he has brought into existence,
"Listen to these human beings bickering in the
courtroom about ownership and intellectual property!
Their acting is quite good, don't you think?"

Meanwhile, out of the corner of your eye, you catch
Sight of such a *dizzying vast array*
of the copyrights He holds title to,
spilling forth from the inside pockets of His vestments,
that you briefly lose all sense of boundary.

His arm quickly steadies you.
Again you sit balanced on barstool,

a faint smile
lighting up your face,

pondering silently
who the real playwright is.....

all my thoughts

flow from and back to

You

my Sweet Lord !

You are the substance

of every vibration

every resonance

in the mind field

that is me,

which is simply

a "cover" for

~ You ~

Kindly continue to

seduce me back

toward home,

that only secure Place

found in the very

midst of all places

all locales;

that Moment which is

the tiniest component of

Time!

RELENTLESS   (MYSTERY BOX)

Certain Saturday mornings,
a poem begins dictating itself to me with the fervor of a
pesky poodle puppy.
I become distracted.

Unbearable beauty at twilight in Bryce Canyon.
Rapid force of water cascading, near the top of Nevada Fall, Yosemite.
Compact sense of interconnected solid fluidity,
all those people moving through Penn Station Tuesday afternoon.
That wrapping around, LARGE SILENCE, enveloping me one
August afternoon, alone, atop Continental Divide in Colorado.

I noticed early in life that the ocean's tides
relentlessly are changing, never standing still.

Now I find this poem spreading out before me,
a panoramic unveiling of dimensions.

These days I'm caring less about the experts,
how to properly wrap one end around to the other
to attain a continuously completing construction.

I'm discovering it happens on its own
{Please don't ask how...}
a Mobius strip of rhythmic aligned consciousness,
floral patterns of repeating geodesic designs
that cause you, the listener, to taste the essence of the very best

hypnogogic experiences of your life until now.

A feeling, long ago forgotten,
yet, just about to be remembered,
immanently revealing itself within the lines on your palms and fingers.

The way your clothing settles in folds and ruffles as you sit relaxed,
legs crossed, chatting at a tea party.

The bed sheets rippling when you throw them back in a hurry to exit.

All the world's a stage, a sagacious playwright wrote, once upon a time.
It ever is so, even without proper signature.

Your own inner Voice recognizes clearly, *THIS*,
during unanticipated moments of luminosity.

And, what plays across such stage is, at once,
random **AND** *remarkably timed.*

There's a Mystery Box inside every human chest.

When its lid is loosed even briefly,

a Radiance brighter than the Sun shines forth.

The night sky becomes as day.

Fireflies must reinvent themselves.

This Light is so dazzling,

and chivalrous,

that it must obscure itself in verse so as to not blind its viewers,

those who wear the clothing you feel on your back.

Now I note, however,

that this poem is as yet unfinished.

It needs a glaze,   and firing in the kiln.

Can you lend a hand, pray tell?

WILLIAM BLAKE, WHO REACHES BACK

William Blake wrote Little Lamb.

I brush aside all copious spam,

as I reach forth into the next dimension.

William Blake is reaching back

with hands that have so little lack,

the songs they sing are bright and quick with Sunshine.

Mr. Blake, he pushes me.

He feeds me manna, serves the tea,

so forth will spread the spritely cool spring morning!

Mine 'tis now the time to weave,

mine 'tis now to never leave,

the stitching forth four corners of these meadows.

He beckons me, he follows forth.

He points the way to the Star North

and, lo, are left behind these gardens gladly.

When you do hear yon melody,

pick up the sticks and clack them click.

View in your chest for that scene panoramic.

For William Blake is smiling where

the dance your legs will yet to dare,

that jig that shakes the waltz to Gloryland.

The never-ending Joy is seen

behind your eardrums beating clean

as Beauty harks that single sacred soul song.

So now the formula is clear!

Around you Mr. Blake wraps dear

that blanket hymn eternal Hallelujah!

IT BEGINS

the same way it ends:

quite mysteriously!

You are walking into your backyard garden,

or through a portal into the Sistine Chapel.

The hands on the giant clock are moving imperceptibly

yet palpably in their appointed direction.

Someone's fingers lightly touch your shoulder...

You turn.

No person is close, yet the sense of a smile is hovering,

superimposed throughout the crowd.

The afternoon: animated, dragonflies' undulations,

liquid atmospheric waves pulsing on skin surface.

I don't recall where I was going with this poem, nor when it began.

Found today, loose in paperback book, Sufi poems.

Nor is that important I realize,

since all matter is constantly changing form and I am no exception.

There will be a turning: It reliably occurs.

The feel of this Presence is undeniable

and grows stronger as I evolve more harmoniously to it.

No one will care one hundred years from now.

No one will know.

Yet still we proceed and must.

There is a way to crack the Code

and you will slice it cleanly as you persist nimbly.

For all those who understand not this telegram,

please be patient.

The hour is drawing nigh when you will view

Fire in the sky of your mind

and a multitude of scriptures will dance their naked quintessence

before your astonished eyes.

It is good to know the loneliness of Truth,

and all indeed will pass that way in time.

For now, however, bow down sweetly,

as you ponder the spacious gap

between two breaths.

This collection of words is intended as a "section divider,"
a pause in the ongoing action of the eternal becoming of this
LIVING universe. David LaChapelle, an exquisitely elegant and unusually
gifted spiritual teacher who left his body in 2009, once told me
I'm firmly positioned within the Sacred Clown tradition,
but I think he may have been kidding.[6]

Think the thoughts you want to think

And you will multi-color link

To all that you want to appear,

That larger dream that you hold dear.

It hovers close. It's very near.

Pull out all stops. Allow good cheer.

Forgive the grudge. Expect the best.

The Silent Law will do the rest. [7]

chalice

I

am

forever

building

up

the   sides   of   this   clay   vessel   to   shape   and

contain

THAT

BOUNDLESS

LIGHT

which

endlessly

pours

through

spilling

o

u

t

e v e r y w h e r e

ALL OF REALITY

All of reality is but a poem
about to be completed.

This poem is the most exquisite dance
your eyes have ever feasted upon.

This dance, a very fragrant,
continually evolving sculpture,
assembling itself within you,
to your total amazement.

This sculpture vibrates as yet one segment of a vast hologram,
composed of one hundred thousand breath-taking sunsets,
in the mountains
and over the oceans.

This hologram is arising with organic ease
out of the most sonorous
symphony you have ever seen.

This symphony is your birthright,
ripe and eager in its fruition,

as a hand,
smelling ever so much like your hand,
reaches forth to receive it.

Friend,

open your hand,

right now!

GAZE INTO MY EYES

Look at my hands, please.

I am cracking open the egg of a hen.

In it will appear the Empty Quarter,

sub-atomic particles orbiting,

our Solar System before the Big Bang,

your daughter's first blanket.

Also, trillions of smaller eggs.

Close your eyes.

Receive the next egg that permeates your palm.

Crack its shell between fingernail and fang.

Out will flow the placenta and body of your next birth.

Examine gingerly.

Inhale the colors and tastes of that panoramic waterfall

cascading from your wrinkled brow.

Apprehend the aromas wafting forth from those

palaces above your head.

Choose one.

Your footsteps have been echoing in its corridors for millennia.

You are arriving home.

Wrap yourself in the sky for warmth.

Drink from this conch shell,

forged in heavenly furnaces, tuned by earth worms.

You've been simmering upon your reflection for an epoch of ages.

Now is the time to finally fully step into it.

Sit down beside me.

The tears baptizing your cheeks, you'll get used to.

Their tangy yearning,

dredged deep from the oceans of this world,

announces the return of a king.

A SECRET WIND

There is a secret Wind which
breathes us all.

It blows beneath the radar,
filling every crack and pore.

It rises belly up,
then down again,

and issues spark that
pumps the heart.

It fires all the thoughts that flow.
This bridge is spanning all below.

Please learn to feel
that It and you

are only One,
not two, oh no!

—

You'll find yourself in every crack
and every pore,

in every rhyme
and so much more.

And this the when that you will be
way far away from misery,

although the mortal coil will
continue coiling,
then splash, then spill.

But in this NOW,
you'll hear your call.

A secret Wind
doeth breathe us all!

KIRTAN IS A STATE OF MIND

The heart already reclines,
sweetly swinging in its hammock
in the lap of the Divine,
eager to sing out the Name.

This evening will be devoted
to stirring the ingredients of kirtan[8]
into a swirl of delight.

Readings of the mystic poet Rumi
will occasionally be heard,
stage whispered from the audience.

Required only, are your ears and voice,
a set of lungs
and access to the yearning
you keep hidden inside your chest pocket.

They always advertise that this is the best way
to meditate in these modern times.
But I say *BE CAREFUL !*

Something might get loose
that can never again

find a tailor

with a tape measure

b i g   e n o u g h . . . .

SUBWAY STOP

I am here for a short time only,
this subway stop.
Doors opened,
the train spilled out its contents
then was gone.
Please do offer assistance as I sort through all these spools of verse
mixed up in a former rhyme, a mischievous ocean storm,
papers shuffled
blown by shrieking wind gusting long strands of her hair
through galley windows,
lines falling off the page
words losing their way in the surf.
A cat swats the yarn ball from flat table surface,
all over the floor,
rolling as it moves round and round, releasing, this way, now that,
bestowing generous challenge for me,
roiled here in 21st century.

Which line follows this?
Eternal moment, Hawaii's northernmost tip,
alone with vast Ocean no land seen,
looking out these sun dried eyes,

She, this voluptuous Pacific, opened up her dress,
giving me briefly
full view,
her original form
revealed,
all its glory
such curvature, penetrating depth, tangy moaning froth,
undulating heavens heaving seaweed fluid tumult,

her breadth becoming

my breath

up and down

up and down

those minutes stretching centuries.

Then, I was completely gone, absorbed,

my mind merged into Hers.

Tear soaked cheeks of bliss return,

Sun shrunken to sesame seed size
lodging itself, cleverly disguised, hidden in
my heart cave.

The eyes see only what they seek

until the time they seek no longer,

only see.

Now sit silently beside me please,
as we sort through these sunset drenched pages
seasoned with olive oil, basil, Feta, a pinch of yearning.

Which stanza should come next?

Can you hear, faintly, from great long interval,

that symphony approaching?

WE PRAY OUT LOUD

we pray inside

we walk along the praire's tide

we open wide our flaps the heart

we wait for inspiration's dart

we look within the forest green

we cook the food from whence we glean

the smell of satisfied delight

the rustic smell of all that's bright

we work so hard

we think of Thee

we ponder how the Tao drinks tea

we wander in and out of time

arrested thoughts oft turn to wine

thus they can flow inebriate

as they shave down all urge to hate

are there really ten thousand things? [9]

are we supposed to give them wings?

can we say YES to all that's sweet

and all that's sour, all that's beat?

can we allow the Goodness here

to be around us full of cheer?

can we present the Mystery with proof

that we reject the fear

with proof that greatness overflows

our banks with sunlight here we rose

unto the majesty of sight

the still mind's secret joy delight

and now that which began will end

in its right place as we do bend

into the prayer that wraps around

and touches its beginning ground !

a

brief

reminder for you

to come to your senses,

recall / appreciate what is most

important in this ephemeral episode

called your life(time). loved ones, occupation /

service to others, physical health, attunement to

the Unfailing Eternal Divine. there ever is opportunity

and hope. it is never too late. please become Present.

despite everything you think, Present is only NOW.

it's

really

just

that

simple

** Y E S **

THESE THE ROOTS WITH FLOWERS GLOWING

These the roots with flowers glowing.
They hatch naught 'til you are done.

They grow up and down then up now.
They bring nurture everyone.

If it comes that you forget them,
this the plan for you to flow:

Bring your forehead rest on Gaia.
Bow as if true hunger know.

Now let lift of cosmic current
raise you up 'til you're no more.

Then the body mind its business;
Serve the many you are shown.

With palms joining, soles a'planted,
your voice sing translucent Tone.

MULTIPLICITOUS

You proceed by a series of moments, unfolding unceasingly,
sometimes with great rapidity, others, at glacier's pace.

If I call You by Your true name, my Queen, You bow graciously,
then quickly remind me of Your trillion other titles.

I lose track of important aspects of You even as I am extracting
You out of the morass in my mental field, just like pulling a deep
and abundantly rooted weed out of moist loose humus filled soil,
ever so gingerly, mindfully, *but then* it still snaps off,
leaving behind half of its heirs.

You camouflage Your vitality behind statues constructed to
portray Your supple brilliance.
They arrive hardened, touched too often.

You are ever changing, never pausing long enough for the
reporters and photographers clamoring for position outside
Your doors of emergence,
a river running through all of space-time,
a torrent surging forward as a boundless, miraculously evolving
body made up of only itself.

I could query why do You torment, but
You will gently remind me I've asked that before.

What can be asked of this monumentally holy momentum arising
simultaneously from every single point in all of existence?

Who of all those listening to this tale can even begin to pinpoint
what such an unending Mystery could even be?

When I start recording these dictations from You
I always think I know where it's going.

Ha!

Now, again, I flounder.

You are perfect, in your multiplicitous simplicity.

I am a perfectly unfinished version of You,

never knowing Your true dimension,
ever reaching forth for more.

That's how we'll leave it, for now, as I lay my pen down.

You'll draw me back, I'm sure....

For the time being however, I must pretend that I am small.

Why do we pray?

Where does one go?

How should I say

that I don't know?

What is the truth?

When does it show?

Who will find out?

Shall I shout "yo"?

If we do sit

in circle here,

will there appear

Big Buddha near?

I think that we

should eat our food.

Let us now sing

our gratitude.

YOU !!!

Oh You, who have no name,
whisper to me anyway,
that I might shout Your Name
to all the worlds!

Oh You, who have no form,
reveal to me in secret,
Your shape, Your form,
that multitudes might come to see and praise You!

Oh You, who art
myriad beyond the ubiquity of these heavens,
become the simple act of unbidden kindness,
that we might plunge Your deep wells of
gratitude and yearning!

May all our tears of joy and sorrow
be Your baptismal fount,

which circulates these waters ever on,
round and round,
back through
and into Thee! [10]

CONSCIOUSNESS IS DRIPPING HERE TONIGHT

Consciousness is dripping like sweat from every brow tonight.

It turns so sweet.

We have to feed the hungry hordes returning from the day's
hot, hard battles
but they mistake this
Manna as mere bread and wine,
thereby continuing their
zig-zag travels yet another set of cycles.

Few, it seems, are they who recognize the Taste.

The edge of God's large serving bowl is your next step,
so keep your eyes *peeled* and
know *when* to lose your grip.

Which brings to mind this reticence.
What shall I do when such abundance of these telegrams arrives
addressed to my attention in yet another ancient tongue?

Does the grand Calligrapher truly expect all these translations
and by what date due, pray tell?

If it is Your pleasure then, impart to me assistance:
Kabir's grand Benefactor, or another [11]
Holy Guise,
some Fragrance blown mysteriously by wind
through my near windows soon,
I beg.

And *NOW*

back to God's serving bowl,
where we do perch upon its lip.
Instruct in us finesse please,
as we prepare to slip.

This slipping is not falling,
but that which rises high.
A butterfly you now are,
this Monarch is not shy.

And poems can turn suddenly.
Your life can open up.
Alchemical Elixir
is here for you to sup!

The next stage is so close now.
Allow it to reveal
just how that pupa did not know
it **really** made this deal.....

HOW TO LISTEN

Drop your pants,
bare your throat,
place all your cards face up.

Legs and arms uncrossed,
eyes soft,
alert.

Silent,

as full moon
in night sky.

Harboring no agenda,
Anticipating no gain.
Having no dinner plans for later.

Rain,
misting in the mountains.

Inching
forever,

back to the sea.

This is a "section divider".
The instructions are as follows:
Everyone should stand up
and celebrate the next breath,
the next sweet thought,
the next new Moment,
which is yielding us into GloryLand,
that Place we all go around
looking for our entire lives.

FURTHER INSTRUCTIONS

There is a perfect path to follow,

yet it tends to elude even the most worthy.

You have opportunity to walk this royal road today,

this very moment, now, being its only access point.

You must endure despite all distractions,

which are multitudinous in the environment

all about and throughout you.

Stay the current as it flows

and you will taste the Water,

that which resides in and out,

that which buoys you.

No technique will assure Satisfaction,

though you do need a boat to stay afloat.

You must abandon this boat, however, in the proper moment.

More aptly, you'll realize that the boat isn't.

You'll know what this means at the auspicious hour,

that it's not what you think . . .

The Answer floats free of all.

It (the Path, Goal, THAT which is called God, Dharmakaya)[12]

is intimately familiar with each aspect of you, has never not been,

has, in fact, always been imprinted all throughout you.

Thus, tread the path.

There's really no choice!

On the other hand, it's pure delight.

Those who've had the Taste

or heard the Sound of It,

recognize these words.

You others,

will.

PERSIST !

NOM DE PLUME

The ALL shines through each one of us;

It craves to see Itself anew.

It cares not for our story line;

It has a job that It must do.

g

r

a

i

l

There is a colossal landscape that can never be seen.

There is in the back of your throat a nectar to be

t a s t e d ,   r e q u i r i n g   n o   f o o d .

Reach inside the inside to a brightly colored

alpine meadow stretching forth into the heavens.

There, listen to a sound no one has heard.

Step through THAT doorway

as it

swings

wide

open

!!!!!!!!!!!!!!!!!!!!

DOOR OF MY HEART

You sit by the door, waiting for me to arrive.
I enter with determination, missing Your overture.

You disquise Yourself on the inside
in a thousand alluring variations,
yet I mistake You for yet another set of thoughts.

I ask of the Sky, "When will I view my Lord?"
You fly past, a flock in V formation.
I almost notice, yet my contact lenses are so dry
and I blink repeatedly.

I wonder what to wear today.
An impression quickly forms
but I look for greater logic.

Oft enough, I can sense You very close,
whispering lightly on the hairs of my neck,
hovering all about as an unseen, vibrant cloak of air.

My faith increases, though doubt can still overshadow
Your ever slight silhouette.

I speak to others of Your affectionate nature,
even as I question if I am noticed.

My yearning thickens palpably.
Sometimes I fear I'm growing mad.
What is one to do?
Where shall I turn?

I allow my annoyance with others,
who seem to know You not,
to drown out Your tender reassurances.

Desires arise:
They quickly disperse this soft sweetness so carefully
stroking all my skin.

My words nearly form a garland 'round Your neck,
yet once again the petals fall away
to the ground at Your feet.

Is the bonfire below my belly truly building over time?
Will this incense smoke coagulate into the letters of
Your secret Name anytime near to Now, my only Guide?

Please, please appear soon,
while this voice can still sing out Your praises:
My throat has quivered with the Scent of Your body
for so many generations.

Can You kindly grant Your blessings soon?

Do come and enter fully
me
while yet my legs can walk across Your skin,
the Earth,
luscious,
full of Grace,
You've painted with such splendid symmetry.

Dissolve this sense of "me"

as a hundred million drops of rain
are so gently falling to the
dry
beneath,

where I lie

lightly gasping,

praying that my thirst be quenched.

THE LIGHT LEFT ON

If I look

inside at the Orb,

I start seeing many varieties of words and scenes.

This isn't new to many writers,

but, but, it can seem such an affliction.

I'm still wanting to shake out the perfect vision from this whirling,

this rattling of molecules that disturbs balance and can cause

shivers to sweep over the surface of my skin and sometimes

yours too if you happen to be around when I get attacked.

Like toy tsunamis in the sand only the sand is fluid

and a bit thicker than water

and the tsunamis, well, they're waves that ripple

but they come from all sides and insides also.

Just the way your Dutch chocolate frozen yogurt is

melting in the cup as you walk

around town in the evening eating it with plastic spoon.

The inside surface of the Orb, which incidentally is

just under the surface, only its back side,

has reflections of all your past lives and all the places

you've ever traveled this life.

There are answers to questions, any question,

yet they're shuffled terribly messily so it looks like gobbledygook.

And the problem, well, it's not really a problem,

just a nagging truth,

is that you have to spend time alone with yourself in the temple,

your inner sanctum, the so-called secret place of the most high,

to be able to comprehend these hieroglyphic patterns

made of wind and salt, bits of Tibetan prayer flags,

swirls of paint thrown against a canvas with

delicate accuracy from 10 feet away at an acute angle.

I know already, have for a long time, what the answer is,

yes, I really do, only I'm sorting it through

and getting it aligned in this world,

with its languages and customs and established cultures and

evolving artifacts, wobbling busily backwards down, down,

down to a winter solstice singularity early in the twenty-first century.

This epistle isn't about particular dates that are only

temporary stopping points on an endless journey,

even though things are getting way curioser

than any rational mind can image.

But here and now, well, I get distracted and

lose my train of thought,

being mesmerized by all these colorful reflections.

And end up where?

Always the challenge to tie up this end to its beginning,

bringing the twine all the way around to the starting point,

making a circle or oval, some variation thereof...

Those of you who've seen this Orb, please help!

How to convey its secluded enigmas to a listening audience,

who haven't run their left hand around its smooth fragrant contours,

haven't tasted the way it folds into the seven directions to EveryPlace,

how dimensions twist and dance before your eyes

but you can't explain how the odor of pizza and rum relate to

orchids and fresh mown hay...

Well, I'll cut directly to before the beginning.

The deal's this:

You have within you a Universe of multitudinously immense variation,

an implicate order of such boundless beauty and joy,

that you absolutely don't want to attempt fathoming it tonight.

Wait for the proper moment,

your deathbed, maybe when you lose your marbles,

travel to Damascus, *or*

perhaps when you sit quietly still in the darkness

long long long past the point of boredom and terror.

There's no time like now.

It's oh so close.......... Go ahead!

You'll find that someone has left the light on when you arrive.

TRANSLATION

Sometime I will translate into English
the erratic, undulating poetry,
which wafts up like temple incense smoke,
spiraling out from my heart cave.
Spread it forth to many lands,
proclamations carried in the
beaks of birds who know their destinations.

How will I deliver this sermon whole,
as it presses against my lips from the inside,
to the waiting congregations of listeners,
when speeches are crafted in advance,
consumers purchase finished products,
and I am struck with this kaleidoscopically transforming galaxy,
rotating in my throat,
ever fusing meaning into form?

When the large Garuda alights on your balcony,[13]
you will see iridescently gleaming sentences
shimmering forth from its opening beak.

Such unanticipated splendor . . . . .
you'll waver awe-struck,
jaw ajar,
eyes wide open,

sensing somehow that you are peering into that primeval Fire
which spoke to Moses
and sent Rumi whirling,
round and round,
round and round,
in that grandest Reverie
envied by all.

All I really want to do

is

snap photos,

make recordings

of

the

rare fine

poem streams

reigning through the sky,

down the gentle sky,

on and all around

that lustrous fountain

known as **"I,"**

lent to me so long ago,

oh so very long ago.

Such a debt owe I . . .

let me make small payment

painting this lush beauty,

vines from all dimensions,

feeding me,

oh feeding me,

even when I hunger,

even when I cry,

ever as I melt between,

ever as I die.

AGAIN . . .

I crave again to be in the land of King Kamehameha,[14]
even though the portal might be everywhere.

I want to watch those hawks soaring high above rocky outcrops,
there in Summit County, Colorado,
even as I climb upward at 13,000 feet.

I wish once more to commune noiselessly with that sting-ray,
flapping slowly its wings through clear water,
eight feet below my goggled eyes.

That sunrise over Bryce Canyon, decades ago,
tugs at the flaps of my awareness even now.

The time when time stopped,
full of wine,
emerging from bathroom, restaurant in Greece,
those two huge watchdogs I hadn't spotted on the way in
when I'd jumped over the short wall to relieve myself.
How pin-pointed became my awareness,
calculating slow motion retreat across earth surface,
eyes on dogs advancing,
their eyes on me,
lines of invisible elasticity connecting us,
'til sudden dash and leap had liberated my flesh
from immanent, intimate enmeshment with their teeth.

How often has time stopped, opening into the Sacred?
Why do I crave such excessive temperance?
Where is personal history when that deafening silence
pounds in my eardrums as I watch
our central Sun dropping into the Pacific?

Perhaps I'll take a shortcut here:

The mind will never ever succeed in pleasing itself.

Yet maybe
                whippoorwills
                                can!

THE WEATHER MAN

Jalal ad-din Muhammad Rumi, the Mevlana,

(original whirling dervish)

was merely a

wildly gorgeous

tornado,

who touched down

(here on planet earth)

with rainbow

delicacy,

and

then

refused

to

d i s s i p a t e

!

THE TRANSLATOR

It's frustrating.
I receive so many calls for assistance;
I must have gained a reputation as a translator.

Marpa was a translator; [15]
perhaps he can help!

Meanwhile, though, the house in which I live cannot possibly
accommodate all these squirrel monkeys and organic gargoyles
with messages slipping out of their pockets as they swarm about.
Words in alien tongues effervescing forth from their mouths in
visibly beholdable patterns of unbelievably elegant beauty.
Lips which telegraph meaning as they torch your skin.
Throats that gurgle,
just like founts hovering in the air immediately above
your upward facing outstretched palm.
A flame spiring outward and up from the center of your own chest,
rising to a height of fifteen inches out in front of these
window-eyes through which you look.

Consensus agreements of what is "real" are as toys in this
cacophony of enlivened competing stanzas.

"Which immigrant will be processed next?"

"Step forward please."

In a universe of fulcrums and spirals,
one cannot hope for any independence of action.

I'm looking this morning for the right combination
so I can mix my porridge.
I requisition God to come down,
offer to me culinary digestible instruction

just as a leprechaun, reading my thoughts,
shouts interruption from the balcony,

"Why does God always have to
come
down ?"

"Why must we choose between black and white, he or she,
inside or all about?"

And why do I look for Him so oftentimes in outside ritual
as I teeter on the verge of being graced here in my den?

These abounding voices in my head, who do they serve?
Shall they be consigned to secondary spectator status?

Why not proceed as at Burning Man
where no bystanders are permitted and
all must realize their part in the plot that
thickens so steadily as to cause
YOU
to rise
with
(or without)
gluten and yeast

if only

you can pause long enough

to peek out,   for an instant,

your previously closed eyes . . . . .

Can any conclusion possibly come in the middle of this
circus tent as the clowns are spreading out amidst the crowd to the
delight and fear of the children, their parents
and all the hungry ghosts who are
yearning for larger mouths and throats so they can fill their
voluminous digestive tracts that were
designed for voracious worship and awe,
revelation and wonder,

in this timeless cathedral on a small wet planet that is

spinning,

spinning

spinning round like J. Rumi, that spiraling galaxy,

round and round like your dreidel,
the spinning toy top,

which contains your body,

through which your soul is superimposed as a vast hologram
in the very center of all space

all of it spinning then
yet more.

Does anyone really think

THIS
       sacred
             motion
                   ever
                         will
                                 stop?

Did you ever think that snowflakes
are falling to see you?
They crave God's latest brushstroke.
It's fabulous: the view!

I melt upon your skin, dear.
I liquefy that you
will open up those diamond mines
that you hold title to.

These treasures come from inside.
These jewels aren't for you.
They're here to decorate this world
to stir the sacred stew.

In any way that you are you
when you awaken to
the splendor of that Light within,
Look NOW, it's Ever New!

Find a way of *turning*

the present moment

at just the right angle

so that self-existent

Divine Light

is seen

f   l   o   o   d   i   n   g

into the

r   o   o   **m.**

WITHIN THE CENTER LIES A STILL POINT

I'm traveling to the source of the big river my raft floats on
and I see many other colorful characters joining in.
As the Sun rises up early tomorrow morning,
all those who are awakened will dance in circles
on the waters' reflections,
and the resulting ripples will resonate outward
just the way those spiral galaxies do.
Pay attention particularly to the space *within* your breathing,
and you *may* catch a glimpse of that ancient fertile plain
that you are heir to,
referenced by Hafiz,
where the dreidel spins effortlessly and
One sees the Moon perfectly reflected on
the still calm surface of EVERYTHING.

PATCHWORK

on my side of the mountain, poems spring out at me,
from behind sagebrush and blooming gardenias,
as i make my way to market
minding my own business.

crickets sing sweet anthems of long lost friendship
while at night there are visions of ancient battles and
caravan routes under the full moon
and around the far side of the sun.

living is anything but smooth when rivers,
long ago forgotten,
are continually sprouting up in my midst.

there are hordes galloping across central asian steppes,
soon to arrive at theatres in your neighborhood.

one friend has survived gunfire, flood, bionic implant
and now whispers sweet bilingual nothings amidst the ivy.

fifteen french hens will be doing calisthenics surreptitiously
on the street in front of your house.

fifty-five wise gorillas will be camping in your
backyard overnight,
though their tents will be gone
before you rise in the morning to look out the kitchen window.

swift secret swans carrying abundant blessing will
anoint your house
and all you have to do is envision happiness
while wishing that every human being be healthy.

i got tangled up with the Beloved today
on a soft bed of white in the middle of a
meadow of ginger crocuses and wildly singing oysters,
but they provided no disturbance since they can
mingle with a different dimension in the time it takes a hair to
blow an eighth of an inch.

our Beloved was hot,

really likes to carry on,
kisses so sumptuously and
with plentiful poetic passion.

all of creation eagerly awaits our every step.

let us feel

IT

back in between our thoughts,

but we need never to complain,

even

ever

so silently.

very difficult to condense into paragraphs
what has been ages unfolding,

the Light which descends
this very moment into our midst
here in this room.

the time remaining is truly unknown,

yet,

it ever opens up

BEFORE US.

MOTHER OF FIRE

Mother of fire, burn me. [16]

Oh Mother of fire, burn me.

Do it as often as You like.

Do it as often as You will.

Do it very often....

Or constantly!

And if it is Your inclination,

And if it is Your wish,

Spare me . . . oh Thou Merciful Fire!

If you can possibly sneak it in,

Spare me, oh Singeing Flame!

You who sit on both sides of the fire,

You who sit on both sides and within,

Won't you please spare me?
You who know my job description,
You who know my worth,

Pray tell, won't You burn me?

Did I say that?

Oh spare me please instead!

You discern what's good to burn.

You who care what's here to spare.

Won't you have Your Way?

But just remember that I'm weak,

and just recall that I am small,

If it is Your wish.

I guess I leave up to you.

I guess to You I must be true,

So burn me as You wish,

So spare me as You will.

Mother of Fire, burn me.

Oh Mother of Fire, burn me.

This is an intermission, time for tea, aka "section divider."
Here's the assignment: When inspiration spills over the sides of the container,
you'll know you're in trouble. Find a way to direct its flow, like harnessing the
wind via wind mills in the hills. Someday very soon you'll realize you're speaking
a language that hasn't even been discovered yet! Turn around then
right now,
breathe in a deep holy breath,
and fling yourself out into the free fall blue sky of
revelation and joyful amazement!
You'll never ever return to your former bounded life,
and never want to.
Aho!

impressions on waking

very early every morning
the Sun lights a match
to be able to perceive
its reflections throughout
all dimensions

of

the

D

e

e

p

THE TUNE OF THE LORD

The tune of the Lord within you is multi-faceted.
It's dripping from your skin this very instant.

You don't have to go anywhere else to hear it.
(Hint: the categories of the mind are the problem.)

You can't move in a direction other than the one you're moving in.
You can't start from a place other than the one
you're occupying right now.

The salvation you seek is already embedded
within the pattern that you are.
It has to roll out from inside, has to unravel, emerge,
as if you had accidentally dropped a valuable diamond ring at the
very beginning of a long, long runway carpet which had then been
rolled and rolled and rolled and rolled up.
In order to recover your lost treasure,
you will have to unroll the entire carpet.

This is so, so simple, and yet the most overlooked, misunderstood
fact in this vast plenitude you find yourself in.
Which is why there are proclamations in holy books such as
"The Kingdom of Heaven is already in your midst!" and
"The Truth is utterly simple!"

There is absolutely nothing outside of yourself which is
stopping you from being happy, from feeling contentedness,
from manifesting all your skills and gifts abundantly.

When you become attuned to and are expressing your life purpose,

you'll find you understand the truth of all destiny,
the truth underlying all reality, by whatever name you call it.

This doesn't mean it's easy. Doesn't imply it doesn't require hard
work. There may be disruptions in and radical changes to
your current life situation.   Who knows?
There aren't any guarantees it'll happen the way you want it to happen,
the way it appears to have happened to others,
the way your culture thinks it should occur.

The thing is,
you can't be attached to anything!
Absolutely nothing!
This is a radical path.
But, you know what:
You don't really have a choice about it!
You still have to do it.
You absolutely have to "unravel" the particular strand you are.
You must emerge through the portals of your own becoming,
your own unique configuration!
But when you stop struggling with it,
stop fighting with the pattern which is you,
you'll see that the whole sequence becomes quite workable.
It isn't nearly as difficult as you thought it might be.
It simply becomes a matter of taking the next step,
and then the next, and then the next,
unfolding harmoniously as you blossom out into
ever widening circles of becoming.

There *will be* surprises along the way, however,
and some of them may be ABRUPT!

The Heart Does Not Believe

that it cannot receive

the blessing of the love it seeks,

that smooth calm peace which never leaks.

The Heart cannot believe

that it cannot conceive

of rings of happiness content

that spin inside all rules when bent,

That cause the Earth to say "Repent !"

to all whose greed doeth make a dent

in Gaia's noosphere which lent

Itself to us the best is meant.

The Heart will not believe

that it shall not achieve

that harmony abounding where

in all small places we do care

And offer help to all who reach

for their salvation, hands that teach

the joy aglow the hearth we place

inside the center, human race.

WHY DON'T WE

Around mountain campfire
While boiling water for baptismal chai,
I'll join hands with the Maiden,
{She, unborn, undying}
Who gently spews forth the
Myriad dainty wildflowers
Painted with spectrums
Borrowed from the stars,
Across more meadows than you and all your
Ancestors could ever dream of.
{This clever Maiden's got Power, Sight}

As She and I do waltz
Through faintly layered curtains of evening alpenglow,
Majestically maintained by fire and stream,
She'll motion to the deepest aspirations
Felt by all who breathe and dream,
Then whisper with fierce
Tenderness
Direct into my ear,
{Best to listen when She speaks}

"Why don't We do it while you're still alive?"

{She'll offer help, success assured}

{Psst, your aspirations were Her ideas to begin with!}

Don't let your song
(one of a kind)
go unsung!

{all of Creation is enthusiastically listening!!!!! }

MEANDERING FLASH

If poetry is guided by sustained idea,
lingering longer than a millisecond,
can a single drop of rain construct an ocean?

If words are used to paint a canvas pretty,
can the artist trace the thought before it rose?

Pan now to this:

I get brief flashes.

Tremendous, bounteous lightening opening
the black darkness momentarily,
revealing Monument Valley's vast profundity.

Or the exact location of the doorway across the room,
that door which spills out onto the seashore,
the seashore which meanders down the coast,
the coast which wraps itself around your shoulders,
and then continues on into the desert.

The Arabian peninsula, Saharan outback,
Joshua Tree, the barren secret places on Mykonos.

Why is all this so?
What does that last question even mean?

Why do large raptors fly the way they do?

How did that monstrous archetypal eagle
arise out of my back in Hawaii?
From between my shoulder blades,
it subsumed this human form into a 70 foot wingspan,
as it soared throughout the realms of ALL.

What does that eagle have to teach me?
To where does this poem lead you?
What can be learned by examining the edges of this world?

Why are we here?
Who is the "we" that wishes to know?

Ramana has an answer to such riddle.[18]
Or at least a strong persuasion.

His experience suggests the "I" is without boundary,
a seamless encompassing of all that seems.

But then the Buddhists insert that no separate self persists,
without realizing the extent to which their argument agrees.

But what about the punctuation at the end,
especially when the end is ne'er in sight?

Do let me know when you have found the Way.
I'll leave a map with bread crumbs on your tray.

PAINTING your PORTRAIT

Purposely plan a pleasing picture of panoramic positive proportion for your *subconscious mind* to perpetually pause upon which produces a plethoric plenitude of prosperity and panoptic peace.

(I dare ya!)

MY TEACHER USED TO SAY, "REMAIN IN THE CURRENT"

You are learning to walk steadily in
this dimension of Form and Shadow,
where all is the desire of motion, the output of impulse.
Every expression you see outside and
in is but the poetry of Pure Spirit.

The Original Word has no second.

The apparent allowable space is not sufficient
to contain the message that is knocking.
Nevertheless, you must persist with the Translation,
having faith that it will be received.

Be flexible as you progress,
continually revising and updating
the articulation of your goals.
No effort is ever wasted.

This entire phenomenal world is a trick,
a sleight of hand, and yet,
the perfect stage for your becoming.

Don't be fooled!
And don't take yourself too seriously.
Remain ever joyous, loving and grounded in Truth.

**You already are the
Living Waters
you seek to
quench that thirst.**

REJOICE!

NOTES

1) **ETCHED...** — Yahveh, Yahweh, Jehovah, God.
Also, regarding the meaning of "surface": Anything you can
imagine is a "surface." The lining of the small intestine, the
"inside" of a proton, the underside of any membrane. The words
you speak and the thoughts you think are all surfaces. Thus, a
question for you to contemplate: What is the "back side" of a
surface, and "where," exactly, is it?

2) **TAP DANCE** — Here's the story behind the creation of this
"Creation Story." In a reverie I actually saw a word, the word
"Absurd", walk up to me. This, to begin with, was absurd, though
I didn't fully realize it until later, when I began reflecting on the
experience while in "ordinary mind."

Imagine the word vertically, rather than horizontally, arranged,
with the "A" at the top and "d" at the bottom. Anyone who wants
to understand this more completely might want to write it out on
a piece of paper. The orientation of the letters themselves also
was vertical. Thus, an upright "A" is atop an upright "b" which is
atop an upright "s" and so forth. And there is the proper spacing
between the letters, even though they are somehow a single
connected unit or body.

A

b

s

u

r

d

Now imagine little stick figure legs and feet extending from the
very bottom of the "d" and stick figure arms and hands emerging
out of the lower part of the "b." And now place a tall top hat atop
the top of the letter "A."

Once the Word "Absurd" arrives in front of me, it tips its hat, with one of its hands. One of these stick figure arm-and-hands actually takes hold of the hat and lifts it up at an angle in the way many of us are familiar with performers doing that in dance events, musicals, movies, as well as in "real life."

Then, it immediately begins doing a tap dance before me while it is still holding its hat tipped and also after it has replaced the hat atop its head. Then, it spins around, so fast that all I see is a whirlwind, the Word "Absurd" having temporarily disappeared into a whirling [spiral, tornado shape] column of air/wind. Keep in mind, mind you, that this entire "vision" is taking place in the "twinkling of an eye." Then, as the "storm", the whirling tornado column of wind, comes to a stop and is again the visible Word "Absurd", an immediate sense of warmth inside (as a counterpoint to the cold unprotectedness of a "storm") is communicated to me, which is meant to be reassuring. During the entire sequence, the Word "Absurd" is communicating telepathically, "wordlessly" so to speak {yes, I know...}, in an experience heavy laden with paradox, double meaning, humor and affection.

At which point, "Absurd" is laughing uproariously, not at me, not at anyone's expense, simply laughing, and I am being "taught" the value of laughter, the importance of levity, of not taking oneself too seriously, of feeling a sense of appreciation and gratitude, always in a light hearted yet authentic and deeply grounded fashion.

Then it follows that It has produced a tree out of itself; It is "painting" a tree into existence, an ordinary tree, any tree, but I am led to know that there is such grandeur, such special sacredness in this ordinary [deciduous] tree [all trees, any tree] as to be positively inspiring, leaving me awe-struck.

Next, I am led to know that something has been implanted deep within me, something good, wonderful, transformative, positively positive, a "sprouting seed" as such. It hasn't sprouted yet. It is in process, having the potential to sprout, but eternally so, forever springing forth, all without any damage to or disturbance of the integrity of me, my body cavity. It is something mysterious, and under ordinary circumstances impossible, yet extremely potent, that has been left behind, a gift given to me which is now an intrinsic aspect of who I am. Something generic, universally applicable in any situation of need, any circumstance of lack or wanting.

Without warning then, this word "Absurd" suddenly disappears right before my eyes, in a puff! It is gone! No evidence or trace of it or any part of it. However, I am instantly given to know that "It" has entered into or become all things, meaning, literally, ALL THINGS, everything manifest, anything you can think of, anything anyone will ever think of, including all things invisible, such as wind, thoughts, ideas, emotions, behaviors, forces such as gravity, in this "world" we call our home, namely this universe, this Earth, the dimension of Form, any form.

And lastly, I am led to know that we [you and I] are to "bow" to "It" as we move through this world, and since "It" is equally present in all things, everywhere, and in every moment, we are to be in a relationship of respecting, of honoring, of recognizing the sacredness, the specialness of this entire dimension called the Earth with all its peoples, cultures, languages, oceans, mountains, forests, animals, weather patterns, all forces and all cycles.

To summarize, this word "Absurd" related to me in an affectionate, friendly fashion, while doing what it did, with the entire sequence occurring in less than an instant, as I was innocently daydreaming. What would you do?

It wasn't until weeks later, after I had written the experience down as the poem, that it dawned on me that it was indeed a "creation story" that I had "heard / seen." A creation story with a sense of humor, that didn't take itself too seriously, yet covered all the basics and was animated by love and compassion, while implying immense power. A creation story that seemed quite unlikely, even "absurd!"

3) **THE DAMAGE CAUSED BY GOD**– The book being referenced is The Subject Tonight Is Love : 60 Wild and Sweet Poems of Hafiz / translated by Daniel Ladinsky, Penguin Compass, 2003.

Mt. Kailas, also spelled Kailash [elevation 21,778' in Tibet], is a holy mountain in 4 religions, Hinduism, Buddhism, Jainism and Bon, a pilgrimage destination that is frequently circumambulated by serious believers. The mountain is considered to be the center of the Universe, the Axis Mundi.

4) **MEAL PRAYER, BUDDHIST SANGHA**– This was originally composed as a prayer before the silent meal at a Buddhist sangha gathering, some of the lines coming together as I was in process of reciting it. I recall being [pleasantly] surprised when a full two minutes of continuous laughter spontaneously erupted immediately after I finished! You had to be there.

5) **SURFER**– Does anyone remember the surfing movie, The Endless Summer, from the latter part of the last millennium?

6) **[1st Section Divider]**– David LaChapelle website http://celebratingdavid.blogspot.com/ and http://www.lachapellelegacy.org/ This David LaChapelle is much more interesting, in my opinion, than the noted photographer who comes up first in a Google search.

7) **THINK THE THOUGHTS YOU WANT TO THINK**– This poem has appeared under the title "Thought and Law" in the March 2012 issue of Creative Thought (vol. 93, no. 3), the monthly publication of the Colorado Religious Corporation, an arm of the Centers for Spiritual Living, Golden, Colorado. The Centers for Spiritual Living is an international organization, with centers throughout the United States, Canada, Jamaica, etc., that teaches what is sometimes referred to as "Science of Mind."

The **"Silent Law"** refers to the Law of Attraction, also known by other names and terms, that unfailing vibrational mechanism present in all of reality, whereby "like attracts like." It only operates deductively, so that whatever premise, thought or idea you give it, It will take at face value and return to you some version thereof. Also stated in the following: As ye sow, so shall ye reap. For every action, there's an equal and opposite reaction [don't be fooled by the word "opposite"]. What goes around, comes around. The Golden Rule. Refer to SCIENCE of MIND, that mammoth wondrous book by Ernest Holmes. By the way, it really pays to comprehend the full implications of this rather simple, innocent sounding Absolute Truth, no less a law of existence than the law of gravity and the laws of aerodynamics!

8) **KIRTAN IS A STATE OF MIND**– Kirtan, most simply put, is call and response chanting of the names of God and other sacred mantras/bhajans, originally performed in the devotional, bhakti traditions of India. It is described in various ancient spiritual texts of these traditions that during Kali Yuga, the current *yuga* or age we are in, the best and surest way to realize God, to find true spiritual Peace, is not through silent meditation or other spiritual practices, but through kirtan, through singing, using the voice, allowing a direct opening of the Heart and a recognition of the true size of the Divine already fully present Within.

9) **WE PRAY OUT LOUD**– The "ten thousand things," mentioned in verse 34 of the TAO TE CHING as well as other sources, refers to the boundless multiplicity of all forms and beings in the manifest universe. In other words, everything in creation.

10) **YOU !!!** – Originally published in Sacred Journey: the Journal of Fellowship In Prayer / vol. 58, no. 6, December 2007 / January 2008, Princeton, NJ.

11) **CONSCIOUSNESS IS DRIPPING HERE TONIGHT**– Kabir [1440-1518] was a mystic bhakti poet and weaver well known in India, who stitched a seamless path between his native Islam and the Hinduism of his guru, while feeding multiple later rivers of spiritual expression, including Sikhism.

12) **FURTHER INSTRUCTIONS**– "Dharmakaya," you can begin to approach, maybe, from the context.

13) **TRANSLATION**— Garuda, a large mythical bird-like creature of Hindu and Buddhist mythology, who is the mount of Vishnu, and *whose wings when flying will chant the Vedas*! Whoa, dude ! !

14) **AGAIN...** — King Kamehameha (the Great) established the Kingdom of Hawaii in 1810, bringing all the islands under one rule for the first time.

15) **THE TRANSLATOR**— **Marpa** Lotsawa [1012-1097], known as Marpa the Translator, Tibetan Buddhist teacher who brought many essential Buddhist teachings from India to Tibet. His main teacher was Naropa; his best known student, Milarepa.

Burning Man {later in the poem}, of course, refers to the week-long "neo-pagan" festival of Life in the Black Rock Desert of northern Nevada from the end of August through Labor Day each year, celebrating non-denominational community, radical self-expression, superb large and small works of art/sculpture, minimal impact self-reliance in non-human Nature. A cross between the Kumbha Melas of India, Woodstock, the Oregon Country Fair, the [first] Human Be-In (1-14-67) and other benchmark cultural events breaking new evolutionary ground. Do your research on these events and ideas, as you become the fun you seek!

And finally, the "hungry ghost realm" is the dimension of **hungry ghosts** or pretas, described in Buddhist, Hindu, Sikh and Jain texts. These entities are believed to have been greedy, jealous, possessive human beings in a previous existence. They suffer from insatiable hunger and thirst. It is of course entirely appropriate to feel [true] compassion for them, recognizing that their real yearning {the same that all human beings feel} is for Love, Connectedness, Truth, Generosity and Awakening!

16) **MOTHER OF FIRE**— This was originally composed as a song/chant to be sung, with Mata Amritanandamayi (**Amma**, the "hugging saint," amma.org and amritapuri.org) in mind, she who is the purifying and compassionate Fire. "Fire," as one of the Five Elements and as a spiritual ideal, provides "heat" and is what

drives the Awakening of Consciousness to Joy, Beauty and Divine Wisdom.

17) **IMPRESSIONS ON WAKING–** This can be sung as a round. One day very soon, I will make a recording of it as part of an uplifting medley of melody to wake you up, set you into flight and inspire you into delivering the Service/destiny/LifePurpose that is yours to manifest this time around! Yahooooo!!!

18) **MEANDERING FLASH– Ramana** is Bhagawan Sri Ramana Maharshi (1879-1950), a very influential "saint" known for his unusual awakening to divine truth at age 16, who thereafter spent the remainder of his life on or at the foot of Arunachala, the holy "mountain" in Tamil Nadu in the south of India. His earliest teachings are documented in the simple book, Nan Yar? (Who Am I?). The "I" thought is the first "thought," and by engaging in continuous self-enquiry, the practitioner can arrive at the originating point, which is a direct spontaneous total knowing/experiencing of the Self (God, Buddha Nature, supply your own favorite Word). It is best not to speak further here, since speaking tends to encourage conceptualization, which can cause you to end up thinking that you aren't who you really are!

19) **MY TEACHER USED TO SAY "REMAIN IN THE CURRENT"** – **"My teacher"** in the title, refers to Brahmananda Saraswati, aka Dr. Ramamurti Mishra, the founder of Ananda Ashram, Monroe, NY (The Yoga Society of New York) and the author of FUNDAMENTALS OF YOGA and THE TEXTBOOK OF YOGA PSYCHOLOGY (a commentary on Patanjali's Yoga Sutras) and other works. His emphasis on learning Sanskrit, as a spiritual practice, has been central in propagating an awareness of the importance of that magical language in America and elsewhere. While leading us in meditation, he would utter, with his thick Indian accent, phrases such as "Feel It!" (stretching out the word "feel" to include about 6 "e's," while referring to the electromagnetic/ pranic Current in the body system). It was a trip!!

ABOUT THE AUTHOR

Jeffrey C. Starbuck is a poet, psychotherapist, yoga and meditation teacher, workshop leader, spiritual mentor and "Renaissance healer." He has been listening to and abundantly understanding the human mind for decades, while assisting countless individuals in their process of emerging into greater wholeness and a fuller expression of themselves.

He has studied the world's sacred traditions extensively, always being led by the desire to grasp the common thread, that unrecorded yet definite resonance, running throughout. Because of this process of translating, integrating and synthesizing these deepest spiritual and psychological truths, he is able to explain, in plain language, these universal principles, so that the listener, client, friend, student, all can learn to decipher and appreciate the essential strum of existence. "What is That, which, when known, everything else becomes known?"

Certified as a yoga instructor at Ananda Ashram in Monroe, NY, in the last millennium and more recently by the Integral Yoga Institute, he has taught yoga and meditation classes and workshops at many colleges, churches, businesses and yoga centers in New Jersey, New York, and Pennsylvania. He is registered with the Yoga Alliance as an RYT.

Mr. Starbuck holds an MSW from Hunter College School of Social Work. Having done clinical practice in Manhattan and Staten Island, he has maintained a private practice for 25 years in NJ and NY, currently with an office in Kingston, NJ.

He has been richly influenced by his associations with Amma, "the hugging saint," and also with David LaChapelle, the spiritual teacher and author. Mr. Starbuck was given the Sanskrit name "Ramdas" by Brahmananda Saraswati (Dr. Ramamurti Mishra), the founder of Ananda Ashram. "Ram" can be said to be a name of God, while "das" generally is translated as "servant." Servant of God. Most recently, he continues his studies of Truth through the teachings of the Centers for Spiritual Living, aka the Science of Mind.

ACKNOWLEDGEMENTS

This is a page of gratitude, recognizing the following individuals who have contributed to the birthing of this project you hold in your hands.

David LaChapelle, author of A Hymn of Changes: Contemplations of the I Ching, and Navigating the Tides of Change, who was gifted at *seeing* and *calling into existence* while singing (guitar in hand) those magical, three-dimensional stories. **Ananda Foley**, "who had David's back" and cheerfully taught us hula and body prayer.

Mahan Rishi (whose eyes sparkle) and **Nirbhe Kaur**, who endlessly serve and consistently provide a joyful venue. **Albert Dumapit**, who "reads" and moves Energy, after majoring in literature. **Sue Bertomeu Albert**, who asked the key question that finally got this book in motion and insists on having Fun. **Jayadeva**, whose Light is infectiously persistent, and who made room at IYI-P for my poetry. **Robert Rosenthal**, whose suggestion led to the book's title. **Dani Antman**, who was Present when I suddenly perceived within the true size of *the Heart.*

Edwene Gaines, who felt the presence of hundreds of poets hovering all around me, wanting to again gain Access to Voice. The wondrous service (Sanskrit: seva) that **Patricia Weimer** and **Charlie Hess** provided to the Milky Way when they allowed Center Heart to emerge at that dedicated location on Elm Ridge Road. **Anne Walsh** (and the late **Paul Walsh**) and the ongoing monthly mostly Buddhist sangha. **Carol Ann Meier,** who kept asking. **Liam Quirk**, who offered conscious feedback about Consciousness. **Cynthia Yoder** (author of Divine Purpose: Find the Passion Within), who kept saying "Keep writing."

Jill Stein, who liked the poem about Fire Ants and dreamt about the rooms in my house I wasn't yet fully aware of. **Linda Gottfried Mannheim**, who put Bly's Kabir into my hands and voice, while continuing to evolve her dance. **Lauri Shea**, who always said "it'll be fine" and was always thrilled when the wooden Oaxacan animals "kept talking." **Noah Starbuck**, my son, who knows how to weave words into tapestries while continuing to discover the Dharmapala he is.
Lila Starbuck, my daughter, who is continuously emerging into a greater expression of herself, while discovering delight afresh at every turn.

Edward Farrell-Starbuck, my brother, who has come all this long Way with me, while fishing in wild places and ministering to multitudes. **Harry** and **Audrey**, my father and mother, who safely landed me this time 'round in Pocatello, Idaho and also contributed a whole lot more after that. **Lollie Starbuck**, my step-mother, who secretly straddled the dimensions while cheerfully leading the singing.

Jerry Wennstrom, who demonstrated the going out and its return. **Milo Fay**, who (in between brush strokes) encouraged me, by listening, while in Amma's aura. **Samar El-Zein Hamati,** whose spoken Arabic prayers were seen hovering in the air before us. **Jeanette Wolfe**, who articulated the colors, tones and fabric of Reality. **Carlos Hernandez**, who listened long and wrote what he heard. **Judy Gale**, who introduced me to Abraham, Esther and Jerry, WOW! **Karen Kushner**, who tirelessly lives, breathes, walks and talks the Science of Mind (which is really all about Love) while teaching us affirmative prayer!

Virginia Prescott, Deborah McKay, Sanela Solak, Leslie Finke, Linda Rightmire, David Danze, Isabelle Liddle, Tony Giles, Jim Gilliland. Many other beings, as numerous as blooming flowers in the spring: forgive me for not mentioning you by name. The next time, we'll pose for a group photo that will span the Grand Canyon. No one acts independently in this beautiful, magnificently woven World of Interconnectedness! I am so grateful to everyone who has contributed to bringing me to this point, as I am now carried forth by Great Winds across this Sky Realm of ever increasing Wonder. The next precious moment of opportunity is just about to emerge, so

HOLD ONTO YOUR HATS................

www.ingramcontent.com/pod-product-compliance
Lightning Source LLC
LaVergne TN
LVHW011409080426
835511LV00005B/448